DAVID BECKHAM

HEROES

First published in 1997 by
Invincible Press
an imprint of HarperCollins*Publishers*
London

© The Foundry Creative Media Company Ltd 1997 (text)

A CIP catalogue record for this book is available from the British Library.

ISBN 0 00 218823 6

Created and produced by Flame Tree Publishing,
a part of The Foundry Creative Media Company Ltd,
The Long House, Antrobus Road,
Chiswick, London W4 5HY.

Introduction by Noam Friedlander

Main text by Jon Sutherland

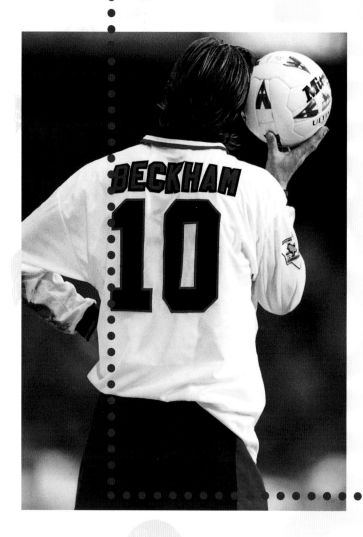

**LAST SEASON** DAVID BECKHAM WAS nominated for the PFA Player of the Year, *Match of the Day*'s Goal of the Season and PFA Young Player of the Year. All this and he's only 22.

Beckham lost out on the first two – after all Zola does have a few more years international experience behind him, and Trevor Sinclair's overhead scissor-kick goal against Barnsley nostalgically reminded viewers of Pele's masterpiece in the classic football film *Escape to Victory*. Nonetheless, this shouldn't detract from Beckham's stunning strike which floated into the Wimbledon goal from the half-way line, on the first match of the season. A truly inspirational goal.

Growing up in London, Beckham started his career as a Tottenham Hotspur Schoolboy, but his fellow team-mates realised that Manchester United held his heart – throughout his training Beckham always wore the Reds' team shirt to match practice. Chased by Tottenham and other Premiership sides, including West Ham, Beckham made it clear that he was holding out for United.

On 8 July 1991 David Beckham achieved his dream – he was signed by the Reds on the same day as fellow England cap Paul Scholes. Their manager, Alex Ferguson, helped nurture the two lads' talents and, building up solid relationships within the team and alongside other youth team members (like the Neville brothers and Ryan Giggs), Beckham has played and learnt with the best.

Beckham continually rises to the occasion, producing the most breathtaking performances. A constant member of Manchester United's trophy winning FA Youth Cup team, with a winner's medal in 1992 and a runner-up's medal in 1993, he was also a crucial member of the England Youth and Under-21 teams, gaining caps from games in 1992 and 1993 against France, Switzerland, Spain and Denmark. In December of 1994, he was in the starting line-up for United's match against Galatasary in the Champion's League – he scored in the 37th minute.

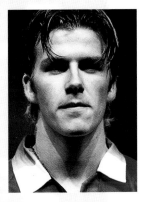

Although comfortable playing in a central role, Beckham can also storm down the right wing scoring sensational goals from free kicks or unselfishly floating in dangerous crosses for his team-mates to pounce on and annihilate their opposition. Together with his inspirational captain, Eric Cantona, it would be no mean boast to say that they were key figures in helping United become the Premier League Champions – again.

After making his League debut at the age of 19 against Leeds in 1995, (his first appearance for United was as a sub for Andrei Kanchelskis in a Coca-Cola Cup tie back in 1992), Beckham has never looked back. The next few years will see him mature into a regular England international, and under Ferguson's wing he'll collect more medals than ever.

'David Beckham has the world at his feet.' You can't argue with Alan Shearer – and he's not the only professional who recognises Beckham's skill, pace and natural goalscoring ability. While some other Man. United players struggled to find their form last season, Beckham never faltered. His popularity, both as a pin-up in teenage magazines and as a player, has meant that he is rarely out of the spotlight. Though his manager tries to protect him from media interference, when under the glare, Beckham always performs with dignity and presence.

*Noam Friedlander*

## FROM THE EAST END TO THE STRETFORD END

**DAVID BECKHAM** IS A tremendously talented and creative young midfielder. He is a hard-working player with a devastating strike and is a deadly accurate free-kick technician. David is the epitome of the success of the Manchester United youth policy. His passing skills are legendary and he seems equally at home either playing for the Reds or for England.

**BORN** DAVID ROBERT JOSEPH BECKHAM in Leytonstone, London on 2 May 1975, he first kicked a ball at Old Trafford at the tender age of 11. David had been drawn to United by his father Ted's love for the club. In the end, this connection would be vital in his career decision to choose United over the many London clubs (including Arsenal and Tottenham) that would be interested in the future. In December that year, as the TSB Bobby Charlton Skills Champion for his age group, he won the coveted prize of a two week training trip with Terry Venables' Barcelona at the Nou Camp stadium. For some years a photograph of David with Terry Venables and Mark Hughes had pride of place in his parents' home in London.

In 1987, at West Ham's Upton Park, he made an appearance as the Manchester United mascot. David finally came to Old Trafford in June 1989 as an associated schoolboy, however, the practicalities of living 200 miles away meant that David did most of his term-time training with London clubs. At White Hart Lane, where he did most of his training at this time, he stood out with his replica United shirts and his burgeoning football ability. It was only during the school holidays that he could realise his dream and take in the reality of Old Trafford at first hand.

*If you stuck a girl or a ball in front of David he'd pick up the ball.*
**John Bullock, David Beckham's school games teacher, *Match* magazine**

*Beckham is unusual. He was desperate to be a footballer. He made up his mind when he was nine or ten. Many kids think that it's beyond them. But you can't succeed without practising – at any sport.*
**Sir Bobby Charlton, November 1995**

**DAVID** was recently asked how Manchester United had heard about him, since he was a Londoner and most of his experience had been down south:

*I was playing for my district team at the time and a scout called Malcolm Fidgeon came over to my mum and asked her if I would like to come up to Old Trafford. Malcolm did a lot for me; he used to take me out training and bring me up to Manchester whenever I wanted to go. I got some publicity for winning the Bobby Charlton skills competition but I was only 11 at the time, so I was noticed more for playing for my district and county teams.*
David Beckham

**WHEN IT** did come to make the move to Manchester, David suffered from all of the typical problems associated with getting used to a new city and living away from home. He had to deal with this when he was just 16:

*I was homesick for the first month or two, but you get used to it once you start playing. The worst time is when you're not playing; that's when I missed home the most. I was lucky to have some brilliant digs. I lived in three different ones, but I liked the third the best. They had Mark Hughes here before me.*
David Beckham, from an interview with *United Magazine*

*....in terms of pure technique, that is control, passing, shooting and free-kick ability, David Beckham is as good as anyone at the club.*
Eric Harrison, United's youth-team coach

**IN 1992** DAVID WAS a member of the team that clinched the Football Association Youth Cup, the first of many honours that would be enjoyed by this emerging talent. David signed on as a professional with Manchester United in January 1993, four months after making his debut as a substitute in the League Cup at Brighton coming on for Andrei Kanchelskis. Having had that taste of first team football, David had to wait for over a season before he had another chance. Later that year, David was part of the United squad that clinched a runners-up medal in the FA Youth Cup.

His first senior start was against Port Vale in the League Cup in September 1994. Two months later, in front of over 38,000 fans watching United go out of the Champions League, he scored his first goal against Galatasaray. The 4-0 victory was the beginning of the signs that Manchester United were beginning to see the fruits of their long-term plans to bring young talent to Old Trafford.

For a time it seemed that David would be over-shadowed by the progress of his new team-mates such as Nicky Butt, Gary Neville and Paul Scholes. Alex Ferguson decided to loan David to Preston North End (for whom he made four full appearances and one as substitute, scoring two goals) for a month in March 1995 so that he could get more first team experience. It was for Preston that David would make his League debut in Division Three against Doncaster Rovers on 4 March. David was back to make his United first team League debut against Leeds that April. David made a total of seven appearances in the 1994-95 season, gradually gaining in confidence.

Two months later, David scored his first goal for Manchester United in their stunning victory over Galatasaray in the Champions League. Unfortunately for United and the four goalscorers, this would be the end of their European campaign for the season. Victory on the European stage still eludes the Reds, but there were great glories to be enjoyed on the domestic front next season.

*It was an experience I'll never forget and to score my first goal as well was unbelievable.*

**David Beckham, on the goal against Galatasaray**

## YOU CAN'T WIN ANYTHING WITH KIDS

**DAVID'S** PRE-SEASON FORM was spectacular, illustrated by the demolition of Newcastle United in the Charity Shield, scoring the third goal in a comprehensive victory against the side that many thought would be the key challengers throughout the season.

The now notorious statement: 'You can't win anything with kids' by Alan Hansen, after United's disappointing showing in their opening match of the 1995-96 season against Aston Villa, seemed to echo many people's feelings that Alex Ferguson had got it all wrong. But how wrong could they all be?

David's fantastic opening strike confirmed his class that had been recognised by Harrison's England Under-21s. Although the next game against Sheffield Wednesday ended as a scoreless draw, David's influence on the game was telling. Showing tremendous first-touch skills that seemed to stick the ball to his feet, his passing and distribution was a joy to behold. Always an unselfish player, David's pass to Scholes in the 19th minute nearly made a goal opportunity. Sometimes David even appears to play like a golfer! Not many players trust their skills and abilities to drive a straight ball to a team-mate, but with his pinpoint accuracy losing possession is hardly likely. So many times in this match, Peter Schmeichel bowled out the ball to David who then took it far upfield, hunting for that telling pass or change of direction that would fool the defence. The trademark stop, look up and change of direction was evident that afternoon. If David had been a foreign import then he would have drawn more attention from the press for his performance, but the newspapers being what they are only commented on the fact that the match did not live up to its pre-kick-off hype.

The press were beginning to notice David, he had the ability and the looks to back it up:

*His slicked-back hair and clean-cut demeanour reminiscent of a cigarette-card legend, Beckham has played wide right for Ferguson, only rarely coming into his favoured central pasture. Thanks to Beckham, the right-wing void created by Andrei Kanchelskis's departure has not become a black hole.*
Henry Winter, *Daily Telegraph*, September 1995

**CLEARLY ALEX FERGUSON** had plans for David, but these were still unknown. In time we would see David installed as one of the mainstays of the United first team, but there was still a great deal of work to be done. Despite Alan Hansen's comments about United, some TV pundits had good things to say about David:

*A really fine player in every respect and he has two feet which a lot of people say players don't have these days.*
Jimmy Hill, BBC1

**TO BE FAIR,** the domestic competition was a bit of a roller-coaster ride for Manchester United and David after the Wimbledon victory, but they settled into three draws with David scoring at the Baseball Ground in early September. Eight goals in the next two games against Leeds and Nottingham Forest and United seemed to be back on track. An uninspiring draw against Aston Villa and then a 2-0 win against Tottenham (both goals scored by the new arrival Solskjaer) was followed by David's brilliant goal in the 1-0 victory at home to Liverpool.

October was the nightmare month for the Reds, conceding 11 goals in the two games against Newcastle and Southampton. The football pundits were already writing-off Manchester United's chances of winning the Premiership. The only consolation was David's goal against Southampton in the 6-3 defeat.

The nightmare continued into November with a poor display by United in their defeat at the hands of Chelsea. The rest of November was a mixed bag of results for the Premiership contenders, two wins, one draw and one defeat. Playing Leicester twice (once at home and once away) in the space of four days led to accusations that Alex Ferguson was not always fielding his strongest side, a 2-0 defeat away was followed by a comprehensive 3-1 victory at home.

December saw the real change in fortunes for the club on the domestic scene, with David scoring twice: once against West Ham in the 2-2 draw, and once in the 4-0 rout of Nottingham Forest towards the end of the month. Two draws and three wins in a month and Manchester United were back on song.

United did not exactly coast to victory at the end of the season, but David was beginning to attract the attention of nearly every club and manager in the country, importantly this included Terry Venables:

*I cannot recall a more promising group emerging simultaneously (David Beckham, Nicky Butt, Robbie Fowler, Steve McManaman, Jamie Rednapp, Gary and Phil Neville). They are the bedrock of England's future.*
Terry Venables, May 1996

**DAVID STILL** had a lot to learn, but Alex Ferguson paid him a great compliment at the end of the season:

*The boy's done an excellent job. He sees himself as a central midfield player, which in time he might just forget about and get on with the job of just playing out there. He's provided great running power for us out there. He's a fit lad, very energetic, got good skill.*
Alex Ferguson, April 1996

*It was also great for David to be compared with some of the United stalwarts:
They [Beckham & Keane] offer aggression, the running power, the defensive qualities, and they also offer goals.*
**Alex Ferguson, April 1996**

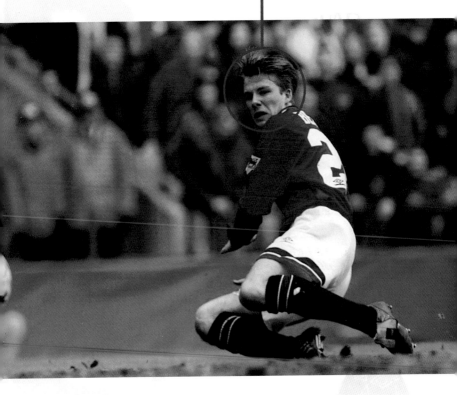

**27**

**BY THE END** of the season
David had managed to clock up
eight goals for United, only four
other players scored more. Eric
Cantona, Andy Cole, Paul
Scholes and Ryan Giggs with 14,
11 and 10 a piece respectively.
His match appearances were
equally as impressive, with only
five players beating David's
gruelling 38 games. This time
they were Peter Schmeichel,
Steve Bruce, Andy Cole, Ryan
Giggs and Lee Sharpe. Perhaps
as a result of the number of
appearances David did manage
to accumulate seven yellow
cards that season.
It had been a tremendous
season for David, a period of
transition between the
newcomer and pretender to a
first team place and a solid
regular with increasing
experience of the game and his
own abilities. Greater tests
would be in store for David in
the summer months.

---

---

## BECKHAM STAKES HIS CLAIM

### THE SPECTACULAR

GOAL BY Steve Slade and David's tremendous performance in the midfield gave England a fantastic start at the Toulon tournament in front of Glenn Hoddle. Clearly, Hoddle was impressed by the performance. The way that David took control of the game from the very beginning; creating numerous openings with intelligent and incisive passing and cutting straight through the Belgian defence with exciting runs, brought the calls for his full elevation to the senior squad to a crescendo.

Setting up the first of England's real chances by beating three defenders with a heart-stopping surging run, this proved to be just the beginning. Moments later he nearly scored in the 35th minute with a beautifully struck curling shot, a certain goal, but denied by the Belgian keeper Ricky Begeyn. David was named Man of the Match.

The England 'establishment' were being made to sit up and listen to the cries that David should be given a full England cap:

*It's nice for us to start with a win and Beckham played very well.*
**Dave Sexton, after the defeat of Belgium in the Under-21 tournament, May 1996**

**EVEN THE** stalwarts of the England squad could recognise quality when they saw it and wanted David into the team as soon as possible:

**31**

*He was always going to be a good player – he just needed the chance to show it. I felt he needed to fill out and become stronger and he has to fight to survive in a club like United. He was thrown straight in but he has proved his quality.*
Paul Ince

**THE MAN** that really mattered was beginning to notice David too. Hoddle was extremely complimentary and had remembered him. It was time:

*He's a good passer and has other attributes, not least a good attitude. The interesting thing for me is that there is a batch of Manchester United youngsters both with the Under-21 and the senior squads who will be playing in the Champions' Cup next season. That will be wonderful experience for them and, from a selfish point of view, bodes well for England.*
**Glenn Hoddle, May 1996**

**TYPICALLY,** the Manchester United supporters had a lot to say about the way in which the England side should be organised:

*He was as magical to watch as usual. Becks has got to be given a full England cap by rights now. How can anyone ignore the fact. He plays like Hoddle used to play and I'm sure that they both know that, now is the time to put the boy out of his misery and get him in the squad.*
**A Manchester United fan, after the Belgian game, one of the many Reds' supporters who also follow the national side**

**THE SUMMER BREAK** was painfully short with Manchester United committed to a number of pre-season games at the end of July and the beginning of August. David's contribution to the first match, against Portadown (away) was a cracking goal that was just one of five on the day. The following day, 28 July, they faced a Select XI and managed another victory, this time 4-1. Inter Milan came next and then Ajax, both encounters proving that the Reds still had a lot to learn about European opposition. Sadly, they both ended in defeats. David and United were back with a vengeance when they demolished Nottingham Forest on 4 August with goals from David, Brian McClair and Phil Neville.

The second week of August saw two big games, first United had to face Newcastle in the Charity Shield match and then Inter Milan again two days later. David not only scored against Newcastle at Wembley, but he also made positive contributions to the other three goals. Unfortunately, United were to fall against Inter Milan once more, but with a more modest score-line of 1-0.

*Don't cry for me Kevin Keegan.*
Manchester United fans, to the tune of 'Don't Cry For Me Argentina' sung every time Newcastle lose to United

**THE UMBRO INTERNATIONAL TOURNAMENT** had placed further pressure on a United side that relied on relatively inexperienced players who had not yet learnt how to pace themselves over the extended playing season. There were calls after the 2-1 defeat against Ajax for a rethink. Despite this, David was probably United's most impressive player. He managed to add intelligence, concentration and strength to his work when seeking the ball. He was also very stylish when he had possession.

*The individual players who impressed me most were Beckham, who was man of the match for me on both days, and Butt. Beckham was everywhere and looked on fire.*
**Manchester United fan, after the Umbro Pre-season Tournament August 1996**

**ALEX FERGUSON** had strengthened United over the summer and with the arrival of Karel Poborsky and Jordi Cruyff (son of Johan Cruyff), David's place in the first team looked a little precarious. Perhaps Alex Ferguson had a longer-term role for David? Certainly he knew that David was too good a talent to leave on the bench. There were other pressures too, David had proved himself to be a future England international and just how Alex Ferguson planned to use David throughout the season could well influence Glenn Hoddle's World Cup plans. The season certainly looked to be one of promise. Glenn Hoddle did indeed intend to call up David for the England squad. After two seasons representing England at Under-21 level, it was time to make the transition to a full senior cap. Clearly, Glenn Hoddle is a great supporter of David and the call-up was recognition of the fact that David had already impressed the England coach and would continue to do so throughout the domestic season. David's first cap would come in September 1996, when on the first of the month he stepped out in Moldova as part of England's campaign to qualify for the 1998 World Cup.

## 1996-97 THE GOLDEN SEASON

**AT THE** BEGINNING of the season Manchester United seemed to have a great deal to prove. The first game promised to be a hard one against the Premiership's dark horses Wimbledon. On the face of it, the Selhurst Park clash was ill-matched; there was a huge difference between the Londoners and United in terms of both price and talent. David took his opportunity, scoring one of the most talked-about goals of the season. It was Manchester United's 300th in the Premiership. Although the goal was not a typical United effort, the impudence and accuracy of David's lob was incredible. Spotting the Dons' goalkeeper, Neil Sullivan, off the line the outrageous shot glided in from beyond the halfway line. David played well that day and nearly scored from a free-kick in the 57th minute.

David seemed to look stronger, sharper and had more of a presence than the last season. He knew, and Manchester United knew, that the footballing world would be looking at them through a microscope for the rest of the season. Everyone had to perform well, always, and at maximum efficiency. Even Alex Ferguson knew that good results would rely on the abilities of David and the other key players in the first team.

The Rapid Vienna game in the Champions' League at the end of September showed the world that Manchester United were capable of mixing it in Europe. They ran rings around the Austrians with David and Ole Solskjaer scoring one apiece. David's range of passing skills and ball control seemed unlimited that night, he was eye-catchingly impressive. So often, the Rapid defenders simply did not know how to handle him with attacks coming in on the left, the right and through the centre of the park, they were being constantly pulled out of position. The first goal started with David and ended with Solskjaer. Feinting a pass to the left, David deftly passed the ball to Roy Keane. Keane was able to gallop into the space left by the deception, then make a diagonal charge and pass to Poborsky. He missed it, but Ole Solskjaer right-footed it into the net.

David's goal confounded his critics and delighted his fans. He has often been labelled as a 'soft' tackler of the ball, but not on this occasion. The hapless Peter Stoger stroked the ball back to the Rapid keeper, Michael Konsel, but under hit it. Certainly the dogged pressure from United had a lot to do with the mistake. David dashed in on the ball and entered the penalty area. Konsel managed to block the first shot, but with a delicate flick David sent the ball past the sprawling Austrian.

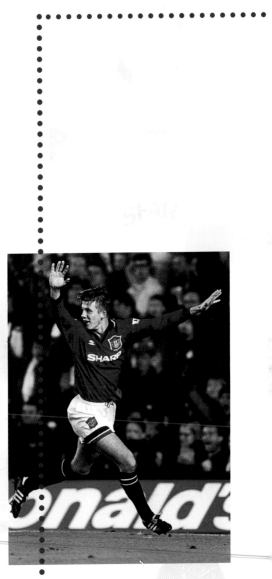

**MEANWHILE,** the Premiership contest ground on, with regular contributions from David:

*Another fine goal by Beckham (does the lad ever score an 'ordinary' goal?) left us gasping – he seemed to have all the time in the world, you could see him look up and decide exactly where in the net he wanted to place the ball and then slowly lifted the ball up over the keeper and into the net.*
Manchester United fan, after the Nottingham Forest game, December 1996

**WHEN DAVID** was made Young Player of the Year at the Professional Footballer's Association annual dinner in Park Lane, the signs of fatigue from a hard season were beginning to tell. David had been a tired-looking figure in Dortmund the week before and had only come on for the last few minutes of the Blackburn game. Largely due to the foresight of Alex Ferguson and the size of the United squad, the luxury of being able to rest young players such as David are possible. Nevertheless, the comments made about David by some of football's giants were enthusiastic and very complimentary.

*He began the Premiership season with a classic from the half-way line against Wimbledon at Selhurst Park. At West Ham, artfully digging the ball from under his feet, he scored again. At Tottenham, he slashed home a beauty from 25 yards. And now this, a glorious shot, the product of athleticism and timing. Frank Sinclair headed Gary Neville's chip into the air and Beckham waited, leapt and struck the ball in off the underside of the crossbar.*
Patrick Barclay, after the draw with Chelsea, *Sunday Telegraph*, February 1997

*I have improved a little bit but I've still got a lot to learn as well. At the start of the season, we'd had new players into the United squad and I was wondering whether I'd get as many games as I did last year. But I have done and I've enjoyed every one.*

**David Beckham, February 1997**

*I don't think you realise quite how good he is until you play alongside him. He can do so many things with a football. He's got the world at his feet.*

**Alan Shearer, winner of the Player of the Year, on David Beckham, April 1997**

*David's got everything, a big heart, big engine and scores great goals. I played against him when he made his debut two-and-a-half years ago and it was obvious that he would be special. But David has the top manager to keep his feet on the ground and he has his dad here tonight. Someone said there are not many youngsters around, but Manchester United has got five of the best: David Beckham, Nicky Butt, Paul Scholes, Ryan Giggs and Gary Neville.*

**Peter Beardsley, winner of a Merit Award for his outstanding contribution to football, on David Beckham, April 1997**

**THE SEASON** brought a hatful of goals for David against a variety of opposition in the Premiership, the FA Cup and the Champions' League. After the pre-season goals against Portadown and Nottingham Forest, plus the goal in the Charity Shield match, David scored regularly and consistently as his confidence and skills improved. He scored against Wimbledon (August), Derby County (September), Rapid Vienna (September), Liverpool (October), Fenerbahce (October), Southampton (October), West Ham United (December), Nottingham Forest (December), Tottenham (January, twice: once in the Premiership and once in the FA Cup), and Chelsea (February).

## PLAYING FOR ENGLAND

**ALL OF** THE SQUAD WERE under tremendous pressure to get results both in Euro 96 and the crucial up-coming qualifiers for the World Cup. With Glenn Hoddle at the helm, in place of Terry Venables, the new manager was casting his eyes around for the talent that would bring continued success to the much criticised England set-up. Hoddle certainly had a good basis upon which to build, the performances had been good during Euro 96 and with the likes of David playing well, he could hope for even better.

*I came across David a couple of years ago when I took Chelsea to Old Trafford and I earmarked him down as a great talent then.*
Glenn Hoddle, August 1996

**IF NOTHING ELSE,** David's contribution to the defeat of Wimbledon made the case for his inclusion in the England squad. On the eve of that decision from Glenn Hoddle, it was clear that United knew this possibility and were making plans.

*David is very young and there's a long way to go yet. But I think he can handle it (a full England cap) all right. We'll just nurse him the way we have been doing. He'll miss a few games. He certainly won't play them all. We'll have plenty of games to play and I'll make changes, especially around the Champions League time.*
Alex Ferguson, August 1996

**EVEN THE** Wimbledon manager could not help but comment on David's goal and the effect it had on his team at the time:

*The keeper ended up with egg on his face. He told me he thought the shot was going over the crossbar. It was wonderful imagination and execution on Beckham's behalf, but our keeper looked a bit silly.*
**Joe Kinnear, August 1996**

**THE** clues were getting easier:
*....that door has been opened now for a few people and they've got to take the opportunity that is there.*
**Glenn Hoddle, August 1996**

*He's learning fast.*
**Glenn Hoddle, after his first week with the England squad at Bisham Abbey, September 1996**

*Matthew Le Tissier has got immense talent, he's shown that to everybody in the last few years, and in international football I think you need very highly technical players, which is the reason why Beckham and Le Tissier are in.*
**Glenn Hoddle, August 1996**

**DAVID'S CONTRIBUTION** to the Georgian game was not insubstantial, he managed to make his presence felt in all parts of the pitch and particularly with his exciting crosses and runs at the defence.

UMBRO

ENGLAND

7

*Crossing in any match is vital. We've got good crossers. Young David Beckham is one of the best technical crossers you'll see.*
**Glenn Hoddle, January 1997**

**HODDLE WAS** not playing hard to get, but he realised that David still had some things to learn and was not about to bring him into the side before he was really ready, certainly not in the role of a central midfielder:

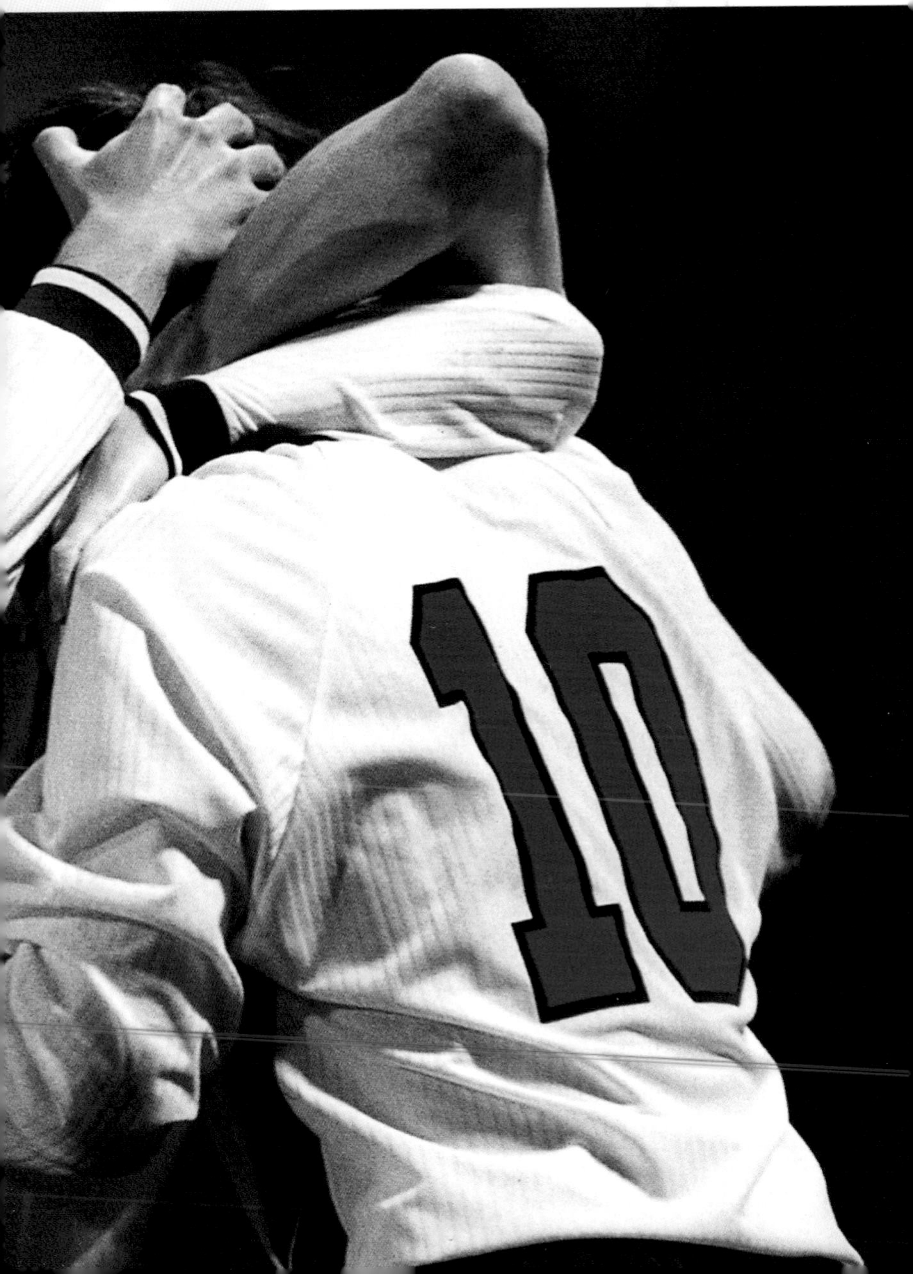
10

*He's still at a tender age. To bring him in at 21 and put everything on his shoulders would be wrong. When he's got 10 to 15 caps, then we can switch him to a more central role. But that's talking long term. I want him to be relaxed and I want him to go out and play. He still has to find his feet.*

**Glenn Hoddle, February 1997**

**WITH THE** domestic season over, it was time for the pundits to look back at the year and assess the key players that they had been looking at for the past 10 months or so. David came in for some very glowing comments:

*Beckham's delivery of a ball, from a set-piece or open play, has been among the season's highlights, as have his swerving finishes.*

**Henry Winter, selecting his team of the season, *Daily Telegraph*, May 1997**

**DAVID'S RAPPORT** with Glenn Hoddle obviously helped him to settle into the new role, particularly given the fact that he was not playing in the same position as he did at Old Trafford.

*I realise that the manager doesn't want to put someone with only five caps into such a crucial position in the middle of the pitch, but I'm quietly confident that I could cope. It's a huge compliment when someone like Glenn Hoddle says I could do that job in the future because he is someone I have always admired. He's compared me to himself at the start of his international career, but I'd love to be even half the player he was.*

**David Beckham, May 1997**

*The experience of playing top quality opposition in different countries can only help me develop and I'm sure Alex Ferguson would not want me to miss out on that.*
**David Beckham, before the summer tournament in France, May 1997**

*I prefer playing in the middle but I'm happy to play anywhere if it means I get a game for England. I certainly don't mind playing on the flank. My first half performance against Georgia was probably my best so far for England. If I get the chance I want to play for England against South Africa, Poland and then in the summer tournaments against Italy, Brazil and the French.*
David Beckham, May 1997

**THE ITALY GAME** in June 1997, with goals from David's team-mate Paul Scholes and Arsenal's Ian Wright proved to be an outstanding game for David. Glenn Hoddle was impressed, indeed he was *very pleased*:

*It was a very good result. We played very well. We enjoyed it and I was very pleased. We played many youngsters. It was a great opportunity for young players to jump at the chance of selection with the World Cup coming up.*
Glenn Hoddle, June 1997

**THE SUCCESSES** that Glenn Hoddle had enjoyed at Chelsea were based on experimentation and the use of younger players as and when the situations presented themselves. The new England manager was fully prepared to use this blue-print for the national team.

*There have been cries for him to play in that position and there will probably be more after this.*
Glenn Hoddle, after the victory over Italy in the Tournoi de France, June 1997

## YOUNG GUN

**AT THE START** OF THE 1997-98 season, Manchester United had strengthened the squad with the likes of Henning Berg, the Norwegian international. Alex Ferguson realised that to mount another claim to the Premiership title and the equally coveted selection of trophies on offer, he would have to maintain the freshness of the side that lapsed at certain times in the previous season. Ferguson's intentions were clear, even the key players like David would have to fight for their place in the first team and would be rotated around if they looked as though they were losing their edge and fitness. Burning out the 'young guns', as the likes of David, Paul Scholes and Gary Neville have been dubbed, before they can reach maturity constantly occupies Ferguson's mind. The manager's experience at Aberdeen, when he successfully challenged the dominance of Celtic and Rangers, was marred by the numerous players who became physical wrecks in their twenties.

*I can add Beckham when I feel the time is right – maybe in about two or three weeks.*
**Alex Ferguson, August 1997**

*Some players want to play every match and I can understand that, but that does not mean I accept it. If we are going to challenge seriously in all competitions we have to maintain a freshness throughout the entire squad and I think my younger ones are now beginning to realise that. They are learning that they will have their share of the big games.*

**Alex Ferguson, August 1997**

### DAVID'S TEAM-MATES,

notably Roy Keane the skipper, rallied around the benched midfielder and the other 'young gun' Gary Neville. However, the interesting coincidence about the first two games of the season was victories over Tottenham and Southampton only after the introduction of David as a substitute.

Becks's a young lad and hopefully he understands the gaffer's position. We've got a big squad and Becks has got to remember that he will probably be involved in the World Cup at the end of the season, if England qualify. Alex Ferguson is a manager, he makes decisions and he has got the option of leaving Becks out of the team if he wants to.

**Roy Keane, August 1997**

It wouldn't have mattered to me who scored the goal, but David did take it very well. I wasn't going to wait too long in the second half before bringing him on because there was no attacking spread in our game and it was too much to expect Dennis Irwin to defend and also to provide us with crosses from the right flank.

**Alex Ferguson, August 1997**

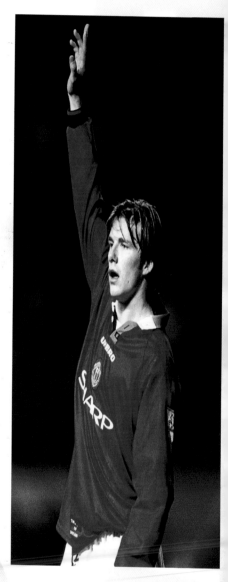

**WATCHING ON** the sidelines can only be a temporary measure and at the very least it does show that Alex Ferguson believes that David will be wearing an England shirt at some point in the season. This is not, however, compensation for the eager Beckham and he must view this period as rather unsettling. Each game that begins without David on the pitch is another tense and awkward time for the young man, he has never been able to occupy himself fully without a football nearby.

*Beckham was the best player on the pitch (again). He was the only one who seemed committed to at least trying to get the ball but he does need protecting from some of the more 'physical' players in the Premiership.*

**Manchester United fan, after the Blackburn Rovers game, August 1996**

*The game itself was a real ding-dong battle. End to end, blood and guts. Beckham ended a great move by belting a cheeky Cantona pass first time against Seaman's post with such force the goal must have been vibrating for some time afterwards. I looked around after that shot and everyone had their heads in their hands in disbelief. It was a great build up finished off with a typical drive from Beckham.*

**Manchester United fan, after the Arsenal game, November 1996**

*Giggs had an amazing chance when a great cross by Beckham fell perfectly for him about 6 yards out with just the goalie to beat.*
Manchester United fan, after the Rapid Vienna game, December 1996

*The rest of the team also looked below par but still managed to put Beckham down the right wing early on for him to send over a pin-point accurate cross to the advancing Giggs who somehow managed to header the ball directly at Ian Walker.*
Manchester United fan, after the Tottenham game, January 1997

*Beckham stepped up then curled the ball over and around the Spurs wall and into the top left corner leaving Ian Walker with no chance whatsoever. Cue mass hysteria as 48,000 reds realised with just eight minutes left the game was over.*
Manchester United fan, after the Tottenham game, January 1997

*An excellent cross from Cole to Scholes got us the first goal and then Becks put in his now obligatory wonder goal! At this rate, the goal of the season is just going to be a list of Beckham goals.*
Manchester United fan, after the Tottenham game, January 1997

*Beckham and Giggs both had good games with some excellent link-up play and good distribution.*
Manchester United fan, after the Coventry game, March 1997

*The other person who impressed me more than on TV was Beckham in that he does a lot of running off the ball, getting into space, particularly to bring the ball out of defence.*
Manchester United fan, after the West Ham game, May 1997

**DESPITE ALL** of the applause and cheers on the day and the favourable comments in the press, this 'young gun' had to adapt gradually to the pressures and the demands of Premiership football at a club the size of Manchester United. As David said, it was a gradual process and one that could not be hurried:

*The pressure of playing was at its most intense in my first few games and then gradually it became less. After my debut I didn't think the games would get easier, but they do. I seem to get less nervous in games this season, which has helped me a lot.*
David Beckham, on pressure at Manchester United

**BECKS**

**'BECKS'**, AS HE IS KNOWN by team-mates and fans alike, is undoubtedly one of the most exciting footballing talents of this decade. Despite the hype and the association with Posh Spice, David remains an uncomplicated and dedicated sportsman. David remains blissfully ordinary, he is gifted and self-assured; seemingly untroubled by his England appearances. He is able to play in the centre of midfield week-in-week-out for United and on the right for England. He does not seem to have any preference or problem with either role. David is an instinctive player, reacting well to situations as they present themselves. Perhaps this is why Glenn Hoddle has so much time for him, after all this is the England manager's approach too. The ability to analyse your own game, rather than dwelling on what the opposition might or might not do to stifle your game, is an attitude that accords well with David's manager when he is in his England shirt.

**WITH AN** impressive collection of medals for one so young, indeed enough to satisfy a player who had been in the game far longer than David; a Football Youth Cup winner in 1992, runner-up the following year, Premier League and FA Cup winner in 1996 along with the Charity Shield and then the Premiership and Charity Shield double again in 1997. There can be no doubt that further honours await him. His awards from the pundits, fans and his peers are equally as impressive. He was named Carling Premiership Player of the Month in August 1996, Sky Sports/Panasonic Young Player of 1996, the Sky Sports/Panasonic Fans' Footballer of 1996 and perhaps the most coveted prize of the Professional Football Association's Young Player of the Year for 1997. Before all of that, we should not forget that the first piece of silverware was the Football Association Youth Cup way back in 1992.

So what about this young, eleven-stone-two six footer? He seems to be able to cope admirably with the pressures and there are only two minor misdemeanours worth mentioning. He was accused of diving and trying to get the referee to book the Austrian player in the Rapid Vienna game. David has never passed a comment on the matter. The other accusation, that he has denied, was the small case of youthful over-exuberance when he, allegedly, mooned at the Southampton fans at the Dell. For the most part David is a clean player with far more interest in the ball than any intent to maim or hurt anyone.

Excluding the 1997-98 season, David has managed to clock up 84 appearances with United with an impressive strike rate of about one goal every fourth game (20 goals so far). The appearances began way back in 1992 with that away game against Brighton and Hove Albion in September.

**DAVID'S** view on football is simple and has always remained the same:
*All I want to do is play football.*
David Beckham, May 1997

**THERE** are times when it just gets too much:
*Being at a club like United, you get well-controlled by the manager and people around you. I don't understand why I'm on the front pages. I'd rather be on the back page.*
David Beckham, on his looks and Posh Spice, June 1997

**APPARENTLY,** after the Sheffield Wednesday game David and Ryan Giggs made up a foursome with two of the Spice Girls, since then David and Posh Spice have been seen together on several occasions. There are even rumours that the two are to be married, but this may be too early to tell. David has also been connected with the Italian Stephanie Lyra, a Vogue model.

Despite all the hype, David's first thoughts are of the game and his performances, on the odd occasion his concentration has got the better of him:

*As the manager said, I open my mouth a bit too much to the ref. It's nothing to be proud of. But it's just the heat of the moment. I'm not an aggressive person.*

**David Beckham, after being booked for fouling Albertini in the 2-0 win against Italy, June 1997**

**IN THE END,** there is only one thing more important than life: *I dream a lot about football and a lot of them have come true.*
**David Beckham**

*It's football. I'll watch any football.*
**David Beckham, when asked whether he likes watching Italian football on TV**

*It does astonish me a bit to see some of the goals go in. But I've always been able to score goals from Sunday League and youth level and reserves and I've had the chance to do it in the first team this year. Fortunately most of them have gone in.*
**David Beckham, February 1997**

*I do pinch myself because you've got things around you, material things, that you'd never think you'd have at 21.*
**David Beckham, February 1997**

**DAVID'S EXPERIENCES** of professional football and the pressures that come with the calling are typical of the many other young players entering the game for the first time. At times he has been confused with all of the attention that he has attracted, but his story of the early years serve as a reminder that football is just like any other job and has its own pressures and new things to cope with and make the necessary adjustments. Except when this happens:

*My God, it's David Beckham! And it is, coming up the steps towards us with his mum and dad. I'm pushed unceremoniously aside as the son and heir races down the steps, shakes a rather embarrassed-looking Becks by the hand, congratulates him on his recent form. He then returns to his seat and mutters about never washing it again.*

**Manchester United fan, during the Coventry City game in which David did not play, January 1997**

**WHEN THE REDS** love you, they really love you and there's no getting away from that. David would never want to.

*There's only one David Beckham!*

A familiar chant at Old Trafford and wherever United play

## BECKHAM, MANCHESTER UNITED & THE FUTURE

**PLAYING FOR** A HIGHLY RATED side such as Manchester United does not come without its share of problems. Obviously, the competition for places in the first team is intense and to some extent that aspect of the situation proves to be as much a problem to those who are invariably on the team list as to those who rarely make it. By the end of the 1996-97 season, David had become one of the casualties of just too many games.

The 'fixture madness' had claimed yet another victim in David; some said that the young lions had become slaughtered lambs. It had been an exciting and intense season for David and the attention he was attracting had almost reached pop-star status.

**DAVID WAS ASKED** in a recent interview about the choice he made a few years ago about joining Manchester United: *I was at Arsenal and Tottenham over the same period, one day a week each, and at the time I preferred Tottenham. The newspapers blew it all out of proportion that Terry Venables, who was the manager at the time, ignored me and that's why I didn't join them. I actually spoke to him a few times, but I always wanted to play for Manchester United because I had supported them since I was young.*

David Beckham, in an interview with *United Magazine*

## DAVID BECKHAM

*It's got a bad state of affairs when I have to rest a player who should be out there enjoying himself.*
**Alex Ferguson, April 1997**

*David Beckham, England's most exciting emerging talent, is the latest to go into protective custody.*
**William Johnson, *Daily Telegraph*, August 1997**

**AT THE BEGINNING** OF THE 1997-98 season, Alex Ferguson had been expected to rest David for a few games in order to ensure that he was fully fit. At Southampton on 13 August, Manchester United were having little success in penetrating the well-organised opposition. Alex Ferguson brought on David 10 minutes into the second half (to replace Paul Scholes) and he immediately made an impression. About 15 minutes from the end of the game,

David almost fashioned a breakthrough when he leapt to meet a cross from Phil Neville. With some 12 minutes remaining, following a tantalising run by Ryan Giggs, David was well-placed to drill home a left-foot shot that would ensure that the 100 per cent start remained that way.

Whether Alex Ferguson chooses to use David in this way throughout the season remains to be seen, but there are many who will be concerned about the number of games to be played. This is particularly true this season with the Premiership, European competitions and World Cup qualifiers for the likes of David.

David does love Manchester United, Old Trafford, his manager and the fans. Since they are the ones that troop out in all weathers to see the Red Devils play up and down the country, it is fitting that the last comments go to them. Sometimes the comments are not complimentary, but mostly they are, and rightly so, as David is one of the products of the successful Manchester United 'system', and now he is a symbol to all who dream of following in his footsteps. There are few that could compare to David, given his young age, but those that do bear comparison are those who have remained in the hearts of football fans despite the colour of their strip each Saturday.

*Cynical fouls on Beckham are commonplace. If you can't stop him legitimately, kick his legs out from under him.*
**Manchester United fan, a common criticism of the ways in which some players attempt to deal with David's ability**

*As the team came out there was a big cheer for Beckham's return.*
Manchester United fan, after the Nottingham Forest game, December 1996

*Beckham's goal – as the radio presenter said, he had time to sign autographs whilst he prepared for the shot! I wouldn't swap Becks for five Shearers.*
Manchester United fan, after the Nottingham Forest game, December 1996

*Every player came in for some treatment, with Giggs, Beckham and Poborsky getting the worst of it. I came out of the ground disgusted by what I had seen and heard. Once back on the bus, I realised that mine wasn't an isolated experience. All around the ground, fans had been giving this sort of abuse to the players and this must contribute to the difficulties players face when they are not playing as well as they could. What does it do to a young player like Beckham to be idolised one minute and sneered at the next?*
Manchester United fan, after the FA Cup Fourth Round Replay against Wimbledon, February 1997

*Poborsky then came on and although he gave the ball away had a major impact when chasing a lost ball, winning it back then passing it to Johnsen who passed the ball to Beckham. You all know what happened next! He ran unchallenged for about ten yards then from nearly thirty yards let go a fizzing drive that swerved into the top right hand corner leaving Walker rooted to the spot for the second time in a week. The celebrations in our section were wild to say the least.*
**Manchester United fan, after the second Tottenham game, January 1997**

*United won a corner at the Kop End with Beckham sending in a teasing cross. Pallister rose unchallenged like a salmon and headered the ball into the net. And yes, as you can imagine the scene in the United end had to be seen to be believed. Absolute bedlam!*
**Manchester United fan, after the Liverpool game, April 1997**

*Yet again Beckham put in another cracking cross that was headed goalward by Ronnie Johnsen only for David James to produce a great, and rare, save and push the ball over the bar. Beckham took the resulting corner and once again Gary Pallister rose like a salmon at the near post and nodded the ball into the empty net to send the 3,500 reds into total raptures.*

**Manchester United fan, after the Liverpool game, April 1997**

## FACT FILE

- *Full Name:*
  David Robert Joseph Beckham
- *Height:*
  6' 0"
- *Weight:*
  11st 2lb
- *Born:*
  2 May 1975 in Leytonstone, London, England.
- *Career:*
  As a junior, Beckham was a regular for the England Under-21 team.

**Manchester United**. Beckham starts as an Associated Schoolboy in June 1989 (aged 14). In July 1991, he is signed up as a Trainee. In 1992 he appears in his first senior match (as a sub in an away match). On 21 January 1993, he is signed up as a Pro.

PL 28 appearances (9 subs, 7 goals); FLC 5 appearances (1 sub); FAC 4 appearances (1 sub, 1 goal); FL 4 appearances (1 sub, 2 goals); Others 3 subs (1 goal).

## BECKHAM'S GOLDEN MOMENTS

- *December 1986*
  Starting young, at the age of 11, David Beckham kicks his first ball at Old Trafford: he is the TSB Bobby Charlton Skills Champion for his age group.
- *1987*
  An exhilarated, 12-year-old Beckham appears as Manchester United's mascot for an away game at Upton Park.
- *June 1989*
  David starts his training at the famed Old Trafford ground as an Associated Schoolboy.

- *8 July 1991*
  Recognising a good thing when they see it, Manchester United sign David Beckham as a Trainee.
- *May 1992*
  Beckham achieves his first honour – as part of the Manchester United Youth side who win the FA Youth Cup.
- *23 September 1992*
  Beckham makes his senior debut for Manchester United in a match against Brighton & Hove Albion (a). He comes on as a sub for Andrei Kanchelskis in the second half.
- *21 January 1993*
  Following his great match performance, David Beckham is no longer a Trainee – he signs as a Pro for Manchester United. From Schoolboy to Pro in three-and-a-half years! Beckham is 17 years old.
- *September 1994*
  Beckham makes his first senior starting appearance. He plays in a match against Port Vale in the League Cup.
- *March 1995*
  Alex Ferguson loans David to Preston North End for a month. Fergie says he hopes this will help Beckham to gain more experience. In his short time at Preston North End, Beckham appears five times, scoring twice.
- *4 March 1995*
  Beckham makes his League debut, in Division Three, for Preston North End v Doncaster Rovers.

- *2 April 1995*
  Beckham's League debut for Manchester United v Leeds United (h).
- *August 1995*
  Manchester United make a disappointing opening against Aston Villa in the first game of the season, prompting Alan Hansen's comment that 'You can't win anything with kids'.

- *December 1995*
  After a disastrous first half to the season, United begin to get back on track, annihilating Nottingham Forest with a final score of 4-0.
- *May 1996*
  By the end of the season, David has chalked up eight goals for Manchester United.
  Unfortunately he also has seven yellow cards to his name.
- *December 1996*
  The Professional Footballers' Association's Young Player of the Year is named as David Beckham.
- *April 1997*
  Beckham sets up a superb goal helping to defeat opponents Liverpool.
- *28 July 1997*
  With Beckham on board, Manchester United achieve a 4-1 victory over Select XI.

## GREAT GOALS

- *November 1994*
  Beckham realises a life's ambition as he scores his first goal for Manchester United.
- *June 1995*
  David scores a supremely memorable goal for United in their victory over Galatasaray in the Champions' League.
- *December 1995*
  Beckham scores twice – once against West Ham, and once against Nottingham Forest (the final score is a 4-0 victory).
- *1995-96 season*
  David notches up a total of eight goals for United. His most important strike was v Chelsea at Villa Park in the FA Cup semi-final. His goal took United through to their 14th FA Cup final.

- *September 1996*
  Manchester United prove to the world that they can take on Europe, by defeating Rapid Vienna. Beckham and Ole Solskjaer are United's goalscorers.
- *12 October 1996*
  More excited Man. United fans as David Beckham scores to beat the Premiership leaders, and constant rivals, Liverpool.
- *27 July 1997*
  In a pre-season away game against Portadown, Beckham puts away a fantastic goal – one of the overall score of five.
- *August 1997*
  Manchester United fans go wild as Beckham scores against Newcastle at Wembley.
- *13 August 1997*
  Despite intentions to rest Beckham for a while, he is brought in to replace Paul Scholes in the game against Southampton. Beckham hits a left-footer home, starting the 1997-98 season as he means to go on.

## BECKHAM & ENGLAND

- *May 1996*
  While playing v Belgium in the England Under-21 squad, Beckham makes his mark once again – setting up several great runs, and kicking a sure-fire goal that was *only just* saved by the Belgian keeper. He is named Man of the Match for his performance.

- *August 1996*
  At the age of 21, David Beckham is selected to play for England. Manchester United's manager, Alex Ferguson, tries to stop Beckham from playing on account of his youth. The national team wins through and Beckham is signed up.
- *1 September 1996*
  Beckham has his full international debut for England v Moldova (a). The game is Glenn Hoddle's first match in charge of the national team.

**89**

## BECKHAM'S HONOURS

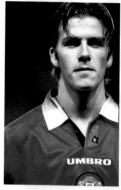

- Beckham wins the 1986 TSB Bobby Charlton Soccer Skills Champion for his age group. The prize is a two-week trip to train with Terry Venables' Barcelona side.
- David is part of the 1992 FA Youth Cup winners' team.
- Beckham's team are the 1993 FA Youth Cup runners-up.
- As a teenager, David plays a vital part in the England Under-21 squad. In May 1996, he is named Man of the Match, England Under-21 v Belgium.
- December 1996 – wins Young Player of the Year.
- Carling Premiership Player of the Month in August 1996.
- Sky Sports/Panasonic Young Player award winner of 1996.
- Sky Sports/Panasonic Fan's Footballer award winner of 1996.
- Wins the 1996 Premier League trophy.
- 1996 winner of FA Cup trophy.
- 1997 PFA Young Player of the Year.
- 1997 Charity Shield winner.
- 1997 Premiership and Charity Shield Double winner.

## HIGH POINTS

- 33 (3) League appearances
- 8 League goals
- 1 FA Cup goal
- 84 appearances with Manchester United, 20 goals
- 9 full caps

## BECKHAM THE CELEBRITY

- By the tender age of 22, Beckham already has three lucrative sponsorship deals: Brylcreem, Adidas and Sondico.
- David is often seen around town and on the front of tabloid newspapers with Spice Girl Victoria Adams. As a result he has become a regular pin-up in teen magazines.
- In August 1997 David Beckham gains the dubious honour of being voted "Britain's sexiest man" by readers of *Company* magazine.

## MANCHESTER UNITED

- Ground: Old Trafford, Sir Matt Busby Way, Manchester M16 0RA
- Ground capacity: 56,387
- Pitch measurements: 116 yd x 76 yd
- Year formed: 1878
- Previous name: Newton Heath LYR
- Nicknames: 'The Reds' or 'Red Devils'
- Greatest score: 26 September 1956, Manchester United beat RSC Anderlecht 10-0 in the in the European Cup.
- Due to damage suffered by Old Trafford in the Second World War, the club took to playing home games at Maine Road for several years.
- In 1957, United became the first English club to play in Europe. They reached the semi-finals of the European Cup; a performance to be repeated in 1958.
- Over two seasons (1956-57, Division One & 1958-59, Division One) United scored two identical totals of their record number of League goals – 103 goals, twice!
- 1958 saw disaster strike United, when eight players were tragically killed in the Munich Air disaster. Top star Bobby Charlton was among the survivors.
- Winners of the European Cup in 1968 – defeating Benfica 4-1 at Wembley.
- The most capped player in Manchester United's history is Bobby Charlton with 106 caps (England).

- Manchester United were the winners of the European Cup Winners' Cup in 1991.
- In 1934, United wore surprise kit – sporting cherry and white hoops instead of their usual red shirts – for the first and only time. They were playing Millwall and won the game 2-0. After the match, the Reds resumed their normal kit.
- David Beckham wears United's No. 10 shirt.

- The record transfer fee paid by Manchester United was the £6,250,000 given to Newcastle United for Andy Cole. The transfer took place in January 1995.
- The largest transfer fee ever paid to United was in June 1995 when Internazionale bought Paul Ince for £7 million.
- Between 1956 and 1973, Bobby Charlton appeared 606 times for United. During these 17 years he scored 199 goals.
- In 1994, United became the fourth team this century to win the double (League and FA Cups). In 1996, they went down in sporting history by being the only team to win the double again.
- Ole Gunnar Solskjaer was the unexpected hero of United's 1996-97 season, notching up a total of 19 goals.
- On 12 October 1996, Manchester United played Liverpool at Old Trafford. 55,128 fans turned out – the largest crowd the ground had seen for 12 years.

Introduction by Noam Friedlander.
Noam Friedlander worked as an intern on the CNN International Sports
Desk in Atlanta. Since then, she has worked on the *Sunday Times* Sports
Desk, *The Box* magazine and the *Manchester United Official Review 96/7*.
She is now a freelance journalist and contributes to *FourFourTwo*,
*Glory,Glory Man United* and Manchester United magazines.

Main text by Jon Sutherland.
Jon Sutherland is an exiled life-long Chelsea supporter who lives in
Suffolk. He has written over sixty books in the past ten years on a variety
of subjects. Although Jon is a great admirer of Manchester United, he
would love to see Chelsea manage the Premiership and FA Cup double!

The Foundry would like to thank Helen Burke, Helen Courtney,
Helen Johnson, Lucinda Hawksley, Lee Matthews, Morse Modaberi and
Sonya Newland for all their work on this project.

Picture Credits
All pictures © copyright Empics Sports Photo Agency except page 80
picture by N. Cairns/The Sun © copyright News Group Newspapers